SUFISM IN NORTHERN NIGERIA: FORCE FOR COUNTER-RADICALIZATION?

Jonathan N. C. Hill

May 2010

*****

Comments pertaining to this report are invited and should be forwarded to: Director, Strategic Studies Institute, U.S. Army War College, 122 Forbes Ave, Carlisle, PA 17013-5244.

*****

All Strategic Studies Institute (SSI) publications may be downloaded free of charge from the SSI website. Hard copies of this report may also be obtained free of charge by placing an order on the SSI website. The SSI website address is: *www. StrategicStudiesInstitute.army.mil.*

*****

The Strategic Studies Institute publishes a monthly e-mail newsletter to update the national security community on the research of our analysts, recent and forthcoming publications, and upcoming conferences sponsored by the Institute. Each newsletter also provides a strategic commentary by one of our research analysts. If you are interested in receiving this newsletter, please subscribe on the SSI website at *www.StrategicStudiesInstitute.army. mil/newsletter/.*

ISBN 1502886375

FOREWORD

Abdul Farouk Abdulmutallab's recent failed attempt to bring down Northwest Flight 253 as it came into land in Detroit, Michigan, has placed the issue of Islamic radicalism in West Africa squarely on the international political agenda. Indeed, his actions and close association with Al Qaeda have raised a number of urgent questions. For instance, what are the chances of further attacks against U.S. interests being planned and launched from Nigeria? Is the country now the latest battleground between Al Qaeda and those who oppose it?

Dr. Jonathan Hill's monograph goes some way to addressing these questions by examining the political, economic, social, and cultural conditions found in the country's Islamic heartland in the north. But it also considers how the threat of Islamic radicalism might be countered, and in particular, the role that the local Sufi Brotherhoods might play in meeting it.

DOUGLAS C. LOVELACE, JR.
Director
Strategic Studies Institute

ABOUT THE AUTHOR

JONATHAN N. C. HILL is a lecturer in the Defence Studies Department at King's College, London, United Kingdom, based at the Joint Services Command and Staff College. He has provided academic support to both the British Peace Support Team (BPST) in South Africa and the British Defence Advisory Team (BDAT) in Nigeria. Dr. Hill has published widely on issues of African security. His most recent book, *Identity in Algerian Politics: The Legacy of Colonial Rule*, was released by Lynne Rienner Publishers in June 2009. He is currently working on a new book, a clutch of articles on Algeria and Nigeria. Dr. Hill holds a Ph.D. in postcolonial politics from the University of Wales, Aberystywth, United Kingdom.

SUMMARY

In light of the ongoing threats issued by Al Qaeda against the United States and its allies, the need to prevent the radicalization of young Muslim men and women remains as pressing as ever. Perhaps nowhere is this task more urgent than in the countries of West Africa. The global expanse of the ongoing war on terror places these territories in the frontline. With large Muslim populations that have hitherto remained mostly impervious to the advances of Islamism, the challenge now confronting the Nigerian government and the international community is ensuring that this remains the case. But in recent years, Islamist groups have been highly active in the region. The aim of this monograph is to assess the potential of Nigeria's *Sufi* Brotherhoods to act, both individually and collectively, as a force for counter-radicalization, to prevent young people from joining Islamist groups.[1]

To achieve this goal, the monograph is divided into four main parts. The first considers U.S. strategic interests in Nigeria. It argues that most of these interests have some sort of security dimension relating to either oil, terrorism, the safety of shipping in the Gulf of Guinea, or the peace and stability of West Africa. In particular, it notes that as the region's key actor, Nigeria can be a vector of either stability or volatility. As such, it is incumbent upon the United States to try to ensure that the country remains as stable as possible.

Section two then looks at the various groups and organizations involved. It opens with an overview of *Sufism* before moving on to trace the histories of the two main Brotherhoods in northern Nigeria, the *Qadiriyya* and *Tijaniyya*. This includes an explanation of the suspicion and hostility that exists between

Sufis and *salafists* throughout the Islamic world and in Nigeria specifically. This antagonism is driven by both theological and political considerations. Yet the Islamist movement must not be considered a unified front, as it is made up a variety of different groups, each with their own agendas and methods for pursuing them. The section finishes with an examination of the means the *Qadiriyya* and *Tijaniyya* use to counter the Islamists' influence.

The third section examines the political, economic, and social conditions in Nigeria — and the north in particular — today. As past experience in other parts of the Islamic world demonstrate, these circumstances are often critical to an Islamist group's ability to expand its membership and propagate its message. While the monograph is at pains to show that the spread of these organizations and ideals is not solely the result of high unemployment and political disenfranchisement, they are clearly contributing factors. And the picture that emerges is indeed worrying, for Nigeria seems to suffer from many of the social ills that have so helped Islamist groups elsewhere in the Middle East and Africa. The main conclusion this section draws is that northern Nigeria represents fertile ground for Islamist groups to cultivate.

The last section outlines the monograph's conclusions before offering up a series of recommendations. Its main suggestion is that the U.S. Government establish a permanent consular presence in the northern city of Kano, Nigeria. Such a mission would act as a focal point through which aid, development assistance, and military training could be channeled. In this way, the United States could extend its influence throughout the entire region and into Niger, Mali, and the southern *Sahel*. This recommendation, like the others the section makes, is designed to limit the spread of Islamist groups and ideas and gradually counteract the political, economic, and social conditions that allow them to exist and, to some extent, thrive.

ENDNOTE - SUMMARY

1. In Arabic, each Brotherhood is known as a *tariqua*.

SUFISM IN NORTHERN NIGERIA:
A FORCE FOR COUNTER-RADICALIZATION?

Introduction.

In 2010 Nigeria will celebrate its half-centenary. The closer the country edges toward this historic date, the more its citizens are drawn to reflect on its past. Few but the most optimistic are likely to conclude that the last 50 years have been anything but difficult. Politically, Nigeria has endured prolonged bouts of chronic instability as time and again the military has intervened to install one of its own as head of state. Far from saving Nigeria from the avarice and corruption of its civilian leaders, the military's actions have helped strangle democracy and institutionalize electoral fraud. Economically, the rapid expansion of the oil industry has enriched a few at the expense of the many as Nigeria has been transformed into a rentier state. Socially, the country continues to be plagued by intercommunal violence as ethnic and religious groups everywhere periodically fall upon one another with murderous intent.

In fact, it is no small wonder that Nigeria has survived at all. The Biafran war of the late 1960s was but the most dramatic manifestation of the regionalist and sectarian impulses that still threaten to tear the country asunder. Even today, the Federal Government (FG) continues to face numerous challenges to its authority. In the south-east, the Movement for the Actualization of the Sovereign State of Biafra (MASSOB) is fuelling and channelling Igbo desires for an independent homeland. In the south-south, the Movement for the Survival of the Ogoni People (MOSOP) and the Movement for the Emancipation of the Niger Delta (MEND) are working in different ways to free this oil producing region from Abuja's control. And in the north, memories of the Caliphate of Sokoto still linger as ordinary people and politicians alike dream of establishing an independent Islamic state of northern Nigeria.

Indeed, of all Africa's anomalous states—and there are many—Nigeria remains one of its most fragile. Yet the difficulties currently confronting the FG are at least partly of its own making. Decades of corrupt, abusive, and inept government have left millions of Nigerians feeling frustrated and desperate. With little faith left in either mainstream politics or politicians, hundreds of thousands of them are drawn to more radical proposals and the individuals who make them. Some of these schemes advocate the complete overhaul of Nigeria's existing political, economic, and social orders. Yet others trumpet the rights of particular ethnic groups. Still others call for the secession of this or that region. Perhaps unsurprisingly, given the prevalence of corruption in Nigerian public life and the selfish behaviour of the country's leaders,[1] these suggestions are often rooted in religion and expressed in moral terms.

It is no coincidence that the past 15 years have witnessed the exponential growth in the number, size, and socio-political importance of religious movements in Nigeria. Within the Christian community (which constitutes roughly 40 to 45 percent of the total population), there has been a proliferation of evangelical and "health and wealth" churches.[2] Among Nigerian Muslims (who make up about 50 percent of the populace), there has been a surge in support for *sharia*, culminating in its reintroduction in 12 of the country's 36 states.[3] In fact, this is one of the clearest examples of religion and faith-based ideas and practices being used politically, even if some of those who called for *sharia*'s implementation were motivated solely by reli-

2

gious conviction. At the very least, its reintroduction is a condemnation of the efficacy of the courts and ability of the state to provide judgment and justice in a fair and timely fashion.

Yet, arguably, this is not the sum of the rebuke being given. Neither is widespread support for *sharia* the only way in which Nigerian Muslims are looking to their religion to express and, they hope, address their political, economic, and social grievances. A number of them continue to turn to groups whose ideas and recommendations are rooted in more radical interpretations of Islam. Such organizations, as they are currently recognized,[4] have been present in northern Nigeria since independence. During that time their individual and collective fortunes have fluctuated wildly. Yet significantly, some have endured and are presently flourishing. Indeed, they are drawing strength from the inability and unwillingness of the federal, state, and local governments to either improve ordinary Nigerians' standards of living, or fully respect their political and civil rights.

In actual fact, based on the experiences of other countries with large Muslim populations in North Africa and the Middle East, the current political, economic, and social conditions in northern Nigeria suggest that the region is ripe for infiltration by radical Islamic groups. But support is also growing, for much the same reasons, for *Sufism*. Represented in northern Nigeria mainly by two brotherhoods—the *Qadariyya* and *Tijaniyya*—it encompasses a rich array of traditions, practices, and beliefs that form a distinct stream of thought and actions within *Sunni* Islam. At times over the past century, this difference has cost those who practice *Sufism* (*Sufis*) dearly. Indeed, both intellectually and, on occasion literally, they have found themselves under attack in many parts of the Islamic world. In the past, a majority of these onslaughts were organized by the various imperial powers as they attempted to retain control of a particular territory. Yet increasingly, these assaults have been orchestrated by other Muslim groups.

This ongoing contemporary wave of violence was originally triggered by the Muslim Brotherhood, which emerged in Egypt in the late 1920s before spreading to other parts of the Middle East and Africa. In particular, the *salafist* tradition it has helped establish and sustain continues to provide the impetus and justification for many of the attacks mounted against *Sufism* today. This tradition, with its call for Muslims to think and act like their earliest forbears (*salafs*), is highly critical of *Sufi* beliefs and practices which, it argues, verge on the heretical.[5] Since then, *salafism* has spread throughout Muslim communities the world over. Perhaps even more worrying for *Sufis*, it has helped give rise and succour to some of the most reactionary and violent factions in the Islamic world today.

Sufis, therefore, including those in Nigeria, find themselves confronted by Islamic radicals. And they are not alone, for many of these groups, again in accordance with their *salafist* beliefs, are also hostile to Western governments and publics. In fact, this threat confronts both *Sufis* and North American and European countries alike. By extension, containing and countering it is a goal they all share. For their part, the *Qadiriyya* and *Tijaniyya* continue to finance and run a range of religious and social programs that have the effect of preventing men, women, and children from turning to these radical factions. To begin, such programs are alternatives to those offered by groups and organizations promoting *salafist* views and agendas.

In addition, they help make up for some of the state's failings, which encourage individuals to turn to radical groups.

Therefore, one of the main aims of this monograph is to examine these programs to assess the ability of the *Qadiriyya* and *Tijaniyya* to counter the radicalization of northern Nigerian Muslims. To sustain this analysis, the monograph is divided into four main sections. The first considers Nigeria's strategic importance to the United States, and why what happens there matters to Washington and the U.S. Armed Forces. This leads, in section two, to an examination of the different Islamic organizations in the region. As well as identifying the size, influence, and make-up of the various radical groups there, the section also provides a brief overview of *Sufism* and the *Qadiriyya* and *Tijaniyya*. It then focuses on what actions the *Sufi* brotherhoods are taking to dissuade people from joining radical groups, and the challenges they have to overcome. The third section then provides an overview of the political, economic, and social conditions in northern Nigeria today. In so doing, it will help determine the potential susceptibility of the region's inhabitants to the radicals' siren calls and uncover the scale of the problems the *Qadiriyya* and *Tijaniyya* have to overcome. Finally, section four offers some conclusions, which it uses to outline a series of recommendations for the U.S. Government and Armed Forces.

Nigeria and the United States.

The United States has a range of strategic interests in Nigeria. Some of them—such as its desire for peace and stability in the Niger Delta—it shares with the Nigerian FG. Others—like its commitment to reduce high-level corruption—are resisted or quietly ignored by the country's ruling elite. Still others —such as its efforts to strengthen democratic institutions and the rule of law—it holds in common with foreign governments and key international organizations. Yet despite these differences in levels and sources of internal and external support, most of these interests have some sort of security dimension. Indeed, it is their security implications that raise them to the level of strategic importance. They have grown in both number and relative significance over the past few years.

To begin with, Nigeria is now one of the world's main oil producing countries. Under the terms of its agreement with the other members of the Organization of Petroleum Exporting Countries (OPEC), it is allowed to pump up to 2.2 million barrels of oil per day. This represents around 3 percent of the total amount extracted daily worldwide, and even though it struggles to meet its quota allocation because of the everyday violence in the Delta, Nigeria remains one of Africa's largest oil producers.[6] Its importance as an energy supplier is raised still further by the quality of the oil it extracts. Described by industry experts as light and sweet, it is ideally suited for refinement into motor fuels.[7] Furthermore, the country's geographic location gives it excellent access to the Atlantic sea-lanes and refineries in both the United States and Europe.

These factors alone would be sufficient to prick U.S. strategic interest, for like its allies in Europe and the rest of the world, the United States is committed to keeping the notoriously volatile global oil market as stable as possible. This means making sure that the flow of oil into it is kept open. And this task is especially important at the moment, given the ongoing instability in Iraq—another major oil producer—and other countries with significant reserves, like Sudan. Yet that is not the sum of the U.S. interest in Nigeria, for the United States is also its best customer, buying 46 percent of all the oil it produces daily. Indeed, it is the fifth largest exporter of oil to the United States, supplying some 11 percent of all the crude the country imports.[8]

To better safeguard this important energy supply, the United States is helping establish a dedicated naval force to improve maritime security in the notoriously dangerous waters off the Nigerian coast. Envisaged as a combined force made-up of U.S., Nigerian, Equatorial Guinean, and British naval assets, the main purpose of the Gulf of Guinea Guard Force (GGGF)—as it will be called—will be to protect shipping and oil rigs from pirates operating out of the Niger Delta. The urgency of this task has grown significantly over the past 2 years as the number of attacks against vessels and sailors has increased.

Indeed, the issue came to something of a head on February 11, 2008, when a Nigerian navy gunboat was fired upon in the Kalaibaiama Channel close to Bony Island after it disturbed pirates who were in the process of attacking a vessel belonging to Total Oil Nigeria. It led the International Maritime Organization (IMO) to warn Nigeria's FG that the country risked being blacklisted if it did not improve security in its territorial waters. Some shipping lines have already taken unilateral action to protect their ships and crews. For example, in January 2008 the Maersk Group suspended all its operations to the port of Onne in Rivers State following an attack on a tanker in Port Harcourt harbour.

Following Maersk's announcement, the Nigerian Vice-President, Goodluck Jonathan, moved to allay the international community's fears by restating the FG's determination to tackle militancy in the Niger Delta. But despite his efforts, on February 12, the International Transport Workers' Federation (ITF) — representing 186 maritime unions with a combined membership of 700,000 people — formally petitioned the main employers group, the International Maritime Employers Committee (IMEC) — representing over 100 shipping firms that together employ around 145,000 people — for crews operating in Nigeria's territorial waters to be paid war-risk bonuses. These waters are now classified as the world's second most dangerous, after the Straits of Malacca. Concerned by the economic and political ramifications of being black-listed, President Yar'Adua gave the GGGF his wholehearted support. Indeed, on January 31, 2008, he and President Obiang Nguema Mbasogo of Equatorial Guinea called for the process of establishing the force to be sped up.

Originally a EUCOM initiative, the feasibility of establishing a GGGF is now the concern of the Gulf of Guinea Commission (GGC), which is made up of representatives from the United States, the United Kingdom (UK), and various countries that border the Gulf, although the final decision whether it will be created or not still rests with each country's government. The main purpose of the GGGF will be to help these countries protect their natural resources, the companies that exploit them, and the flow of oil onto the world market. If the force is created, the United States is likely to provide it with boats, radar, and communications equipment and help train the crews of the participating African navies.

West African support for the proposal has been built up over the past few years. In October 2004, U.S. Naval Forces Europe (NAVEUR) hosted a Gulf of Guinea Maritime Security Conference in Naples at which representatives from 17 navies sought to identify the main security challenges confronting them, as well as highlight issues of common interest. One of the outcomes of the conference was a decision to hold a joint training exercise some time during the following year. On January 25, 2005, the USS *Emory S. Land* began its Gulf of Guinea deployment with 20 foreign naval officers onboard. As well as providing technical assistance to the Cameroon navy and in-port navigation and seamanship training, the men and officers of USS *Emory S. Land* took part in search and rescue and force protection exercises.

While such deployments by the U.S. Navy are not new — it has been conducting training exercises in the Gulf of Guinea since the late 1970s — the proposal to establish the GGGF has given them added importance and led to changes in the types of exercises it undertakes with its regional partners. In the most recent exercise, which began on February 22, 2008, codenamed Exercise Maritime Safari, vessels and aircraft of the Nigerian navy and air force and the U.S. Navy ran maritime surveillance drills. These exercises are important, as they help the United States gain a clearer understanding of what capabilities its regional partners actually posses. Moreover, they also help foster understanding between the U.S. and Nigerian navies and enhance the Nigerians' ability to unilaterally conduct such operations in the future.

Although the military and political benefits of undertaking such exercises may not be profound, they are real. So too are the reasons why the GGGF should be created. The proposed force will benefit the United States by making the Gulf more secure for maritime traffic; better safeguarding the flow of oil from Nigeria and Equatorial Guinea; helping the Nigerian government extend its authority over the ungoverned space of the Delta and curbing the illegal trade in bunkered oil; strengthening its relations with the countries that border the Gulf; and, increasing its military footprint in a region that has traditionally lain outside its sphere of influence. The GGGF will also benefit Nigeria by helping it combat the pirates and water-borne militants who terrorise shipping in its territorial waters.

More specific to the north are the U.S. efforts to limit the area of operations of insurgent and terror groups based in Algeria. The most significant of these is *Al Qaeda in the Land of the Islamic Maghreb* (AQLIM). Known previously as the *Salafist Group for Preaching and Combat* (GSPC), its link up with AQ has breathed new life into its campaign against the Algerian government.[9] Not that this has significantly increased AQLIM's chances of achieving ultimate success. For Algeria's security forces are now adept at dealing with the threats posed by insurgents and terrorists. Indeed, so effective are their counterterrorism and counterinsurgency strategies that they have forced the AQLIM and its fellow travellers to seek refuge in Algeria's vast hinterland.[10]

As a consequence, however, Algeria's neighbours to the south are now exposed to AQLIM as never before. Episodes like the GSPC attack on a Mauritanian army outpost on June 4, 2005, highlight the very real threat this group poses to the governments and populations of the *Sahel* and broader West Africa subregion.[11] It now seems that AQLIM has made it a strategic objective to become more active in these countries. Indeed, it has recently emerged that the group sent agents into Nigeria in June and July 2009 to assist the *Boko Haram* group in its armed struggle against the country's security forces.

AQ's growing influence in this corner of Africa is naturally of great concern to the United States and its allies. Nigeria is important both because it is one of the countries the group is seeking to infiltrate, and because it holds the key to the region's stability. As home to one-in-three sub-Saharan Africans and as a driving force within the Economic Community of West African States (ECOWAS) and the African Union (AU), what happens there is of continent-wide significance. Indeed, its sheer size means that it can project either stability or volatility for many miles beyond its borders. Helping its armed forces and police meet the challenges posed by Islamist radicals, therefore, is absolutely vital to Africa's long-term security, especially given that Nigeria's immediate neighbours include some of the continent's most fragile and vulnerable states.[12] In fact, when two of them (Liberia and Sierra Leone) descended into bloody civil war in the early 1990s, it was Nigeria that led international efforts to contain the violence and protect their civilian populations. It remains one of the largest contributors of troops to the AU force currently deployed in Sudan and is likely to commit a significant number of personnel to the organization's proposed mission to Somalia. For the continent's sake then, it is essential that Nigeria continues to perform these functions. And this means helping it protect itself from AQ infiltration and internal instability.

So it was with the intention of restricting AQLIM's area of operations that the United States set up the Pan-*Sahel* Initiative (PSI) in December 2002. With an initial budget of $7 million, the PSI's primary purpose was to help Chad, Mali, Mauritania, and Niger better protect their borders against Islamist insurgents and terrorists operating out of Algeria. In addition to these funds—which rose to $125 million in 2005—the U.S. European Command (EUCOM) sent the 10th Special Forces Group (Airborne) to Timbuktu, Mali, to establish and operate a training center for units from all four countries. The value of the PSI was confirmed during the autumn of 2004 when these troops played a vital role in helping kill and apprehend the members of a GSPC warparty looking to kidnap competitors taking part in that year's Paris-Dakar rally.[13]

Indeed, this success helped persuade Washington to launch a new program called the Trans-Sahara Counter Terrorism Initiative (TSCTI) in June 2005. With an annual budget of $100 million, it was more ambitious in scope and involved Algeria, Chad, Mali, Mauritania, Morocco, Niger, Nigeria, Senegal, and Tunisia. Its goal remains to help the governments of these countries stem the flow of money, people, and weapons across the porous borders that divide them. Nigeria's inclusion in the TSCTI was an acknowledgement by Washington of both AQLIM's potential reach and ambitions, and of the country's importance to U. S. efforts to contain and combat the group. This recognition has been reinforced by the country's receipt of a significant portion of the military assistance fund managed by the Department of Defense's (DoD) Defense Security Cooperation Agency (DSCA).[14]

Radical Islamic Groups in Northern Nigeria.

Helping preserve Nigeria's domestic stability, therefore, is a major concern for the United States. Although the threat from Islamic radicals is concentrated almost entirely in the north, the consequences of their activities continue to ripple throughout the rest of the country. Every army and Mobile Police (MOPOL) unit sent to the region to contain a demonstration or quell a riot orchestrated by Islamist youths cannot be deployed in the Niger Delta to counter MEND or the other insurgents. In addition to the strain this places on the security forces, there are economic and social costs, such as the financial outlay for deploying these units, the loss of overseas investment, internal population flight, and heightened intercommunal tensions in other parts of the country, to name but a few.

Indeed, and as the heads of the *Qadiriyya* and *Tijaniyya* acknowledge, the challenge confronting them and everyone else seeking to stem the tide of Islamist radicalism is at once both ideological and practical. As crucial to the religious arguments they marshal, are the various community outreach programs they finance and run. For not only do they help mitigate the shortcomings of public services, they form alternatives to those offered by the Islamists. Yet arguably, the Brotherhoods' task is made all the more difficult by their desire to work with the authorities whenever possible. Unlike the Islamists who simply condemn the federal, state, and local governments, the Brotherhoods try to engage with them. Not that the *Qadiriyya* and *Tijaniyya* try to defend the indefensible, as any attempt to do so would certainly serve them ill. Rather, they have to funnel the discontent their members and wider community still feel toward the government in a constructive way.

That the *Qadiriyya* and *Tijaniyya* find themselves both in this position and able to perform this balancing act is due to their standing within northern Nigerian society. The widespread respect they have come to command has developed over the past 2 centuries and is, at least in part, rooted in their links to the Sokoto Caliphate. These ties give the *Qadiriyya* and *Tijaniyya* a legitimacy that is at once local and international, historic and contemporary, religious and political. For although the Caliphate is now not what it used to be, it still has substance and its leaders, the Sultan and various *Emirs*, continue to exert enormous influence.

Indeed, their present standing is testament to just how important the Caliphate was. At its height in the mid-19th century, it covered a huge area that included northern Nigeria and parts of what is today southern Niger and northern Benin. But it was more than a political empire. It was also a religious community, rendered distinct from its Islamic neighbours to the north and west by its piety, and from the animist peoples to the south, by its rejection of heathenism. And at its summit — combining the roles of king and high priest — was the Sultan. Based in Sokoto, he claimed descent from the Prophet Muhammad, an assertion that, rhetorically at least, made both him and his rule beyond reproach. Yet even with this self-declared religious authority, the Sultan still ruled through a series of viceroys or *Emirs*.

Today's Sultan and *Emirs* are descendants of the men who originally seized power in the early 19th century. Yet they do not command the political authority that their forebearers once did. Its erosion began in the late 19th century as a result of European colonial expansion. In the wake of the soldiers, adventurers, and missionaries who extended British and French influence over the West Africa subregion, came colonial administrators. Although not many in number, they formed two impervious layers both above and below those traditional rulers who were allowed to keep their thrones. Although often obscured, theirs was the word that really mattered, backed up as it was by the modern gunboats of the British and French navies. So placed, these bureaucrats set definite limits on what the traditional rulers could and could not do.

Yet, arguably, the final nail in the coffin of the Sultan's and *Emirs'* sweeping political powers was

Nigeria's independence. Given its multiethnic and multifaith citizenry, the country adopted a secular constitution that placed power in the hands of elected officials. Therefore, nominally at least, the Sultan was relegated to the role of upstanding citizen, an aristocrat, and religious leader. Yet, as Nigeria's unhappy history since independence shows, the constitution is often worth little more than the paper it is printed on. So although the Sultan has no formal political powers, his influence is still considerable. Presidents continue to seek both his opinions and his support, for his command of the faithful means that he can make the government of the north extremely difficult if he so chooses.

The Brotherhoods' links to the Sultan extend back to the very earliest days of the Caliphate. Indeed, the first head of the *Qadiriyya* was Usman dan Fodio, the main leader of the *jihad* that established the Caliphate and the original Sultan of Sokoto.[15] In the decades following his death in 1817, both it and the *Tijaniyya* worked hard to spread their influence and recruit new members from right across the newly conquered territory. That they were allowed and even encouraged to do so highlights the high level patronage they enjoyed. Far from being viewed as competitors to the royal authority of the Sultan and the *Emirs*, the Brotherhoods were seen as collaborators in the grand project of renewing and spreading Islam in this corner of Africa.

Although Britain's colonization of the Caliphate helped trigger the long decline in the Sultan's political powers, it was arguably not as disastrous for either him or the Brotherhoods as it might have been. For early on, the British decided that they would rule the territory indirectly. They therefore left the existing political and social structures largely intact. Even though they viewed the *Qadiriyya* and *Tijaniyya* with some suspicion,[16] they still allowed them to continue pretty much as before. It might be argued in fact, that this mild hostility only strengthened the Brotherhoods' credibility among the local population, while Britain's preservation of the Caliphate structures ensured that they and the Sultan retained their privileged positions within northern Nigerian society.

Indeed, far from withering on the vine, both Brotherhoods have prospered. Although there are no accurate figures as to how many members they each have, they are today counted in millions and can be found the length and breadth of Islamic West Africa. This places their current leaders—Qaribullahi Sheikh Nasir Kabara (*Qadiriyyia*) and Sheikh Ismail Ibrahim Khalifa (*Tijaniyya*)—at the head of two religious communities that are as large as they are important. More precisely, they are important because they are large. For when Sheikhs Kabara and Khalifa speak, they do so, nominally at least, on behalf of a great many people whose actions they can influence through example, proclamations, and religious edicts.

Major ingredients of the glue that binds their memberships together are the values and histories both Brotherhoods promote and embody. *Sufi* is an Arabic word that—perhaps unsurprisingly, given its centuries of use—has acquired a multitude of meanings. It is also a value laden term that is employed both in praise and condemnation of certain individuals, groups, sets of ideas, and practices. By and large though, *Sufis* view themselves as "Muslims who take seriously God's call to perceive his presence both in the world and in the self . . . [and] stress inwardness over outwardness, contemplation over action, spiritual development over legalism, and cultivation of the soul over social interaction."[17] It is this commitment to introspection and quiet meditation that has sustained descriptions of *Sufism* as being mystical and esoteric.

Each Brotherhood celebrates the efforts of a particular individual to achieve spiritual self-enlightenment. During their lives these saints, as they are usually referred to, displayed a single-minded determination to live piously that eventually led them closer to God. But in addition to the example they set, the saints, through their daily routines, marked out a path for the faithful to follow. The goal of each *Sufi* therefore, is to emulate their saint, to show the level of commitment and observe the same rituals, practices, rites, and obligations as the saint did. For if they do so, then eventually they too might gain enlightenment and get to know their Maker better.[18]

Usually, the Brotherhoods take their names from the saint they revere. The *Qadiriyya* is named after Abdul-Qadir Jilani, a scholar and jurisprudent who rose to prominence in Baghdad in the late 11th and early 12th centuries. Similarly, the *Tijaniyya* is named after Ahmad al-Tijani, who lived and worked mainly in the western Maghreb between 1737 and 1815. As their origins suggest, both Brotherhoods have spread and expanded from their respective bases in the Arab world. The communities in northern Nigeria and West Africa, therefore, can be considered local chapters of what are truly global movements. And there as elsewhere, the histories of the two Brotherhoods are closely connected. In fact, al-Tijani was at one time a member of the *Qadiriyya*. Yet he left after growing frustrated with what he saw as its rigid hierarchy and failure to provide greater support to the poor. Arguably, his experiences and disillusionment help explain the cool relations that have historically existed between the two

Brotherhoods. Even today in Nigeria, they rarely work together, viewing each other more as rivals than partners.[19]

And in some ways they are, since both Brotherhoods draw their members from the same pool of people. Without doubt, this competition is an unnecessary distraction, as it prevents greater cooperation between them to the detriment of the outreach programs they offer. These would surely be enhanced through the sharing of resources, know-how, ideas, and personnel. Moreover, by working together, the Brotherhoods would better protect themselves from the vitriol and machinations of the Islamists. For the *Qadiriyya* and *Tijaniyya* remain, along with the secular authorities, prime targets of Islamist hatred and anger. Indeed, the *Jama'atul Izalatul Bid'ah Wa'ikhamatul Sunnah* (or *Izala* for short) — one of the most important Islamist groups currently operating in northern Nigeria — was established in "reaction to the Sufi brotherhoods."[20]

In fact, the very name confirms the group's hostility toward *Sufism*, as it means the "society for the removal of innovation and reinstatement of tradition."[21] It is a *salafist* organization that embraces a legalist and scripture centered understanding of Islam. Its goal, like that of other such groups, is to strip the religion of all impurities, of all foreign (and in particular Western) ideas and practices. It seeks to do so by encouraging the faithful to live by its quite literal interpretation of the *Qur'an*, *sunnah*, and *hadith*; to emulate the *salafs*. Its fervent belief in a true Islam means that it stresses uniformity across the *umma*, and is therefore very concerned with its members' social roles and interactions.

Much of this stands in complete opposition to what *Sufis* both believe and practice. For them innovation is extremely important, as it provides the means by which the individual undertakes his or her spiritual journey toward enlightenment. Indeed, the paths set down by the Brotherhoods are the very definition of innovation, as they have been fashioned deliberately to facilitate this passage. But it is not simply their rejection of scriptural and legal specificity that outrages the *Izala*; it is also their veneration of saints. To many *salafists*, this verges on the heretical, as it seems to undermine or contradict the Oneness of *Allah*. For there can be no division of God's glory or omnipotence and neither, on any account, should the faithful worship false idols.[22]

For the most part, then, the *Izala*'s grievances with the *Qadiriyya* and *Tijaniyya* are rooted in religion and theology. Yet clearly, it would not be so distressed if the Brotherhoods' profiles in northern Nigeria were lower. Indeed, if their memberships were small, their influence insignificant, and their views of little consequence, it would be less concerned with what their followers thought and did. It is because they are important that their perceived deviancy matters so much. The *Izala*'s opposition to the *Qadiriyya* and *Tijaniyya*, then, is motivated, at least in part, by what are essentially political considerations. Its concerns are kept alive by the closeness of the Brotherhoods' ties to the Sultan and *Emirs*, as these links preserve their importance and influence.

Indeed, the enduring strength of these relations has helped cement their positions within northern Nigeria's establishment. While this has undoubtedly brought great benefits to both Brotherhoods over the years, it has also left them exposed to further criticism. They are associated with a socio-political order, which, in the very least, has failed to shield the northern Nigerian public from many of the burdens they now have to bear. As a result, it has made them targets of those Islamist groups seeking to enact revolutionary change. Such organizations — which include *Ahl al-Sunnah wal-Jama'ah*, *Ja'amutu Tajidmul Islami* (Movement for the Islamic Revival [MIR]), and *Boko Haram* (or the Nigerian Taliban) — are driven by both religious and political considerations. Or rather, their political opposition to the *Qadiriyya* and *Tijaniyya* is less a consequence of their theological grievances than it arguably is for the *Izala*.

Indeed, the Islamist movement in Nigeria is made up of an assortment of groups that rarely, if at all ever, coordinate their actions. Their reluctance to do so hints at the profound differences that exist between both their respective agendas and approaches to pursuing them. This divergence is at its most stark between the two oldest and best established organizations — the *Izala* and Malam Ibrahim al-Zakzaky's Islamic Movement in Nigeria (IMN).

The *Izala* first emerged in the early 1960s out of an informal scholastic movement centred on the prominent writer, jurisprudent, and preacher, Sheikh Abubakar Gummi. Born in the early 1920s, he first made a name for himself as a critic of British colonial rule. But once Nigeria achieved its independence, he focused his wrath on the Sultan and *Emirs* for allowing what he argued to be the creeping westernization of northern Nigerian society. His views reflected the traditional education he received in Sokoto, Kano, and the Sudan. Indeed, it was in Sokoto that he first befriended Ahmadu Bello, Usman dan Fodio's grandson and the first Premier of Northern Nigeria, and Yahaya Gusau, his fellow founder of the *Izala*.

In 1955, Gummi made his first *hajj* to Mecca. Travelling with Bello, he was introduced to King Saud bin Abdul Aziz, who encouraged his translation of Islamic texts from Arabic into Hausa. This meeting, and the other contacts Gummi made along the way, was to have a profound impact on his thinking and the direction the *Izala* took once it was founded. For while Gummi did not embrace *wahhabism* in its entirety, many of its values chimed with those he held. And over the years, the Saudi Arabian government is reported to have given the *Izala* significant material support and encouragement. These provisions are allegedly made through the Saudi Arabian embassy in Nigeria.[23]

Once Gummi returned from Saudi Arabia his links to Bello helped him gain teaching berths in Kano and Kaduna. He used these positions to continue his work translating the *Qur'an* and *sunnah* into Hausa, and to promote his *salafist* views. Then almost overnight, as a result of Bello's murder by Igbo army officers on January 15, 1966, his animosity toward the Sultan and Emirs, *Qaidiriyya* and *Tijaniyya*, hardened. Bello had been a calming influence on Gummi. And out of respect for his friend, who was a member of the family that had done more than any other to make the Caliphate of Sokoto what it was, Gummi toned down his criticism. But with Bello's death, any brake that had been placed on what he said and did vanished. Indeed, it was very soon after Bello's death that he co-founded the *Izala*. He did so in part in retaliation against the politicians and religious leaders who seemed to either benefit from or care little about Bello's assassination.

Given Gummi's centrality to the group, its membership includes many of his former students and is concentrated mainly in his home-town of Kaduna and, to a lesser extent, in the near-by cities of Kano, Jos, and Zaria. Its division between these urban centres has prevented the creation of a tightly centralized organization. Its disparateness only increased following his death on September 11, 1992. Indeed, he had acted as something of a lynchpin. And even though he was quickly succeeded by his son, Dr. Ahmed Gummi, a highly respected Islamic scholar in his own right, his removal only increased the devolution of influence and authority to local leaders and sheikhs.[24]

Yet even so, the group remains committed to much the same agenda set down by Abubakar Gummi 40 years ago. It seeks to advance the agenda by many of the means that Gummi pioneered. As well as being an active teacher, Gummi made good use of the pulpit to promote his beliefs. From the early 1970s onwards, he appeared regularly on television to comment on religious festivals and issues. Of course, some of this national exposure came to an end when he died, as it was tied to him personally and the result of his reputation as an Islamic scholar. Yet, while it lasted, it helped establish the *Izala* as a definite force within northern Nigerian society. *Izala* members have not shied away from confronting their rivals in the *Qadiriyya* and *Tijaniyya* head on. Numerous times throughout its existence, its young men have clashed with the *Sufis* on the streets.

Yet their methods are not as violent as those sometimes used by Zakzaky's followers. In truth, the IMN is unique among those groups that make up the Islamist movement in Nigeria, as it cannot rightly be described as *salafist*. For while it has a few *Sunni* members — some of whom undoubtedly harbour *salafist* sympathies — it is in the main a *Shiite* organization. Zakzaky's career as an agitator and would-be revolutionary began when he was at university. While a student at Ahmadu Bello University (ABU) in the late 1970s, he became a leading light in the Muslim Students Society (MSS) and helped organize a series of events calling for the implementation of *sharia* law. Eventually, after several bouts of unrest on the Zaria campus, the university authorities lost patience with him, and he was expelled on December 14, 1979.[25]

It was at this point that he dedicated himself full time to promoting the cause of Islamic revolution. And just like his hero, Ayatollah Khomeini, he recorded sermons on cassette tapes that were widely distributed throughout northern Nigeria's major towns and cities. Habitually, these fiery epistles attacked those in positions of political and religious authority — the federal and state governments, the Sultan, the *Emirs* and the Brotherhoods. Indeed, it was the *Qadiriyya*'s and *Tijaniyya*'s links to the northern establishment that marked them as targets of Zakzaky's wrath. His main argument was that the secular authorities were not fit to hold power, and that the traditional religious rulers, either through cowardice or self-serving interest, facilitated their abuses by refusing to stand up to them.[26] Throughout the 1980s and 1990s, therefore, he and his followers petitioned for the implementation of *sharia* law and sought to bring about an Islamic revolution similar to that which happened in Iran in 1979.

As well as circulating recordings of his sermons, Zakzaky and his followers, many of whom were students from ABU and other northern universities, printed newsletters and staged demonstrations. Then in the early 1990s, shortly after the Kano riots of 1991, they created the *horas* or guards. Modelled on the Revolutionary Guards in Iran, these militants were tasked with providing security at group meetings and other events. As a result, they frequently clashed with the police, Christian youths, and the members of rival organizations, including the *Qadiriyya* and *Tijaniyya*, earning Zakzaky a reputation as someone quite willing to use violence to further his aims. It was also over this period, as the creation of the *horas* suggests, that his admiration for both the Iranian model and *Shiite* Islam grew. This was to have a profound effect on his group and the Islamist movement as a whole. Indeed, perhaps the most important consequence was that it alienated many of his *Sunni* followers. So much so, that in the late 1990s one of his most trusted lieutenants, Abubakar Mujahid, left his entourage and founded the MIR. Based primarily in Kano, it adopted many of the tactics used by the *horas* and quickly developed a reputation for causing and exploiting street level violence. And of greater concern to the police and authorities was the capacity of both groups to organize massive protests. Collectively referred to as the Muslim Brothers, they became a formidable grass roots force, "capable of bringing out a half-million people into the streets of Kano."[27] Both Zakzaky and Mujahid are noisy supporters of *Al Qaeda* and Osama Bin Laden.[28]

Of the two, Zakzaky's IMN, as it became known, is the larger organization. His embrace of *Shiite* Islam and admiration of Iran won him influential backers in Tehran. Over the last 2 decades, it has provided him and his group with financial and other support. Indeed, without this help it is highly likely that the IMN would have withered on the vine, given that the overwhelming majority of Nigeria's Muslims are *Sunnis*. As it is, the IMN uses these funds to promote the *Shiite* and Iranian causes through a series of activities including *ta'alim* (study sessions that take place three times a week), *ijitima* (more intensive study sessions), *daura* (seminars and workshops), *khutba* (religious sermons), and *muzaharats* (mass demonstrations).[29]

In fact, Zakzaky's link up with the Iranians has helped give him a new purpose following the northern states' adoption of *sharia* law.[30] For once they did so, one of the main planks of his agenda was removed. Yet crucially, the IMN remains committed to "involving itself in national or international issues that are of concern to Muslims, as well as in solidarity with oppressed sections of the Muslim Ummah such as the Palestinians and Iraqis . . . [and] to mark certain events such as Quds Day and Ashura Day." And more worryingly, it seems quite prepared for the violence that often accompanies these rallies and "sometimes results in heavy casualties on the part of the movement."[31]

Just as the *Izala* does with the funds it gets from Saudi Arabia, the IMN uses some of the money it receives from Iran to build prayer rooms and offer free education to the children of poor families. Indeed, it is alleged that as well as teaching these children for free, both organizations give them food and a little spending money.[32] In light of the widespread poverty found throughout the north and the abject failure of the federal and state authorities to maintain public services, such acts of welfare are greatly appreciated by the recipients. And the poverty of those receiving it helps guarantee their loyalty to the group providing it. Moreover, this investment in schools and education is part of a deliberate strategy to target children and young people.[33]

Unsurprisingly, the *Izala*, the IMN and the other Muslim Brothers proclaimed the introduction of *sharia* a victory for them and their respective causes. Long had they campaigned for its implementation; and for equally long had they seen their efforts thwarted. Its sudden adoption, then, not only seemed to vindicate their patience and persistence, but also represented— so they argued—a first crucial step along the path toward the creation of a truly Islamic society. To some extent, they were justified in their self-congratulation. Certainly their role or influence was not as great as they often claim, but through their actions they have helped bring about its introduction.

Yet, the northern states implementation of *sharia* also presented the *Izala* and Muslim Brothers with some new problems. For a start, it robbed them of an issue they had long used to attack the secular authorities and traditional religious leaders. For many years *sharia* had given them a convenient stick with which to beat their enemies, but now they needed something else. More seriously, it led to the emergence of even more radical Islamist groups, which soon developed huge grassroots followings. The most prominent and successful of these new movements was *Boko Haram*, which in the space of just 7 years has managed to establish itself as a major rival to the existing Islamist groups.

The group, which often refers to itself as the Nigerian *Taliban*, first emerged in 2002 in the northeastern city of Maidugari, which is located close to the borders with Chad and Cameroon. From the outset, and until very recently, it was led by a charismatic young firebrand called Mohammed Yusuf. It was established in direct response to the introduction of *sharia* law. Its implementation helped persuade the 3,000 or so men, women, and children who became the group's original members to emulate the Prophet's *hijara* or flight from Mecca to Medina and withdraw to a remote part of Niger State. They referred to the area they occupied as "Afghanistan" and lived there peacefully for a number of years.

Yet in Borno and Yobe States, groups of young men, keen to either enter Afghanistan or to set up similar communities elsewhere, clashed repeatedly with the police. In the main, they were postgraduate students who had recently returned from studying in the Sudan and were eager to put what they had learned into practice. Indeed, they quickly condemned the existing religious authorities as corrupt and, therefore, illegitimate.[34] Such arguments found a receptive audience among the young urban poor, who had few opportunities open to them and little to look forward to. So much so that the group quickly attracted, if not the outright support, then sympathies of tens of thousands of people in towns and cities across the north.

That *Boko Haram* was a force to be reckoned with first truly became evident in 2004 after its members clashed with police and members of the security services in a series of bloody riots. Throughout the summer of 2009, large parts of the north were plunged into turmoil due to further violence that began in earnest on July 26 when *Boko Haram* militants opened fire on a police station in Bauchi. In response, the state governor called in the army to restore order. Over the next few days it fought running street battles with *Boko Haram* gunmen until it finally surrounded Yusuf's compound. It took several more days of heavy fighting before the insurrection was finally crushed. Latest estimates place the final death toll at between 700 and 800 people.[35]

But even that, and Yusuf's summary execution by police, failed to put an end to the fighting. Even after his death, or perhaps because of it, violence broke out in towns and villages across the north. That it continues to occur is of great concern to the authorities and security forces. Yet even more worrying are the sophisticated nature of the attacks, the use of firearms, and the links *Boko Haram* has allegedly established with AQLIM. Indeed, these attacks were a step up from the riots and other religious violence that habitually grips the north, as they were part of a coordinated strategy to break the government's authority in the region.

The grievances that gave rise to this violence and the popularity of the services offered by the *Izala* and IMN makes the community outreach programs financed and run by the *Qadiriyya* and *Tijaniyya* all the more important. For they represent two of the few alternatives for many poor people living in the north. In both instances, these programs are built around education — schools and colleges, lessons and courses. Today, the *Qadiriyya* runs a nursery, a primary school, a secondary school, and a college that is accredited to award diplomas. Unusually for northern Nigeria, all classes are co-educational. The *Tijaniyya* similarly teaches children and youths of all ages, and also helps adults study the *Qur'an*, and learn to read and write.

Both Brotherhoods are highly active throughout Kano and the north in other ways. In fact, their programs mirror that of the IMN and include sermons and prayer sessions, workshops, seminars, meetings, rallies, and events to celebrate important dates in the religious calendar. But in addition, given their status within Nigeria's religious community, both Sheikh Kabara and Sheikh Khalifa appear regularly on national television and radio. This, arguably, gives them access to a much broader audience than either Dr Gummi or Zakzaky or Mujahid or the leaders of *Boko Haram*.

Ripe Conditions: The State of Northern Nigeria Today.

According to most indices of human development, Nigeria has made little progress over the past

49 years. Moreover, and of arguably greater concern to its citizens and the international donor community, the country has regressed in certain crucial areas. In fact, since 1960, the year in which the country gained its independence from Britain, the amount of people who are functionally literate has fallen, the electricity output of the country's power stations has decreased, the percentage of the population living in poverty has increased, and the divide between rich and poor has grown.

Of course, the rate of this decline has been neither steady in tempo nor consistent in its consequences. Rather, it has occurred in fits and starts, sometimes quicker and more profound, at other times slower and less dramatic. Yet, taken over the course of Nigeria's post-colonial history, it has been unremitting, especially from the mid-1980s onwards. No part of the country has been left unaffected. While some regions and their inhabitants may not have suffered as badly as others — Abuja in particular is a relatively privileged and protected place — none have been spared entirely, let alone bucked the trend of stagnation and degeneration. In fact, nearly all but the wealthiest of Nigeria's citizens have had to endure growing hardships and falling standards of living.

Yet even so, northern Nigeria has been one of the regions hardest hit. Its decline started as early as January 1966 and was triggered by the collapse of the First Republic. For many northerners of an age to remember it, and some who cannot, the First Republic remains the finest incarnation of the post-independence state.[36] That they should still hold such a view is hardly surprising, given the political dominance of the north throughout its existence. Stretching all the way to the southern borders of what are today the states of Kwara,

Kogi, and Benue, the north encompassed nearly two-thirds of Nigeria's sovereign territory and was inhabited by around half of all its citizens. And as a result, its voters were allowed to fill one out of every two seats in the National Assembly.

Indeed, it was the north's large size that underpinned its political preeminence. And the only way the leaders of the other two (later three) regions could constrain it, was by working together, which they seldom did.[37] But in the end, it was the very scale of the north's preponderance that proved to be the First Republic's undoing. Fearful of what they saw as the creeping northernization of Nigeria— the steady spread of both Islam and Hausa-Fulani cultural practices throughout the country— a group of mainly Igbo army officers overthrew the government on January 15, 1966. After arresting and then executing Prime Minister Tafawa Balewa and Premiers Ladoke Akintola and Ahmadu Bello of the Western and Northern Regions respectively, the conspirators handed power to the army's most senior officer and fellow Igbo, General John Aguiyi-Ironsi.

But if they hoped their actions would bring stability and an end to the north's political dominance, they were soon proved to be mistaken. For just under 6 months later, on July 29, 1966, Aguiyi-Ironsi was himself ousted in a *coup d'état* led this time by a cabal of northern officers. They, in turn, installed the army's most senior northerner, General Yakubu Gowon, as the country's new head of state. And in so doing, they helped solidify the process of political succession that had begun with the overthrow of the First Republic, a process that was as violent as it was undemocratic. Indeed, since then, power has seldom been ceded peacefully, and governments have rarely stood down voluntarily. Even during this current, supposedly golden age of Nigerian democracy, former president Olusegun Obasanjo tried to have the constitution amended to allow him to serve a third term in a desperate bid to remain in power.[38]

Although the *coup d'état* that destroyed the First Republic weakened the north's grip on power, it by no means broke it entirely. In fact, of the 11 heads of state who followed General Aguiyi-Ironsi, nine were northerners including the present incumbent, Umaru Yar'Adua. Yet even so, this power did not really benefit ordinary people living in the north. They, like their compatriots in other parts of the country, continued to be largely excluded from the political process. This was certainly the case throughout the long years of military rule. For much of their time in office, Generals Aguiyi-Ironsi, Gowon, Murtala Mohammed, Obasanjo, Muhammadu Buhari, Ibrahim Badamasi Babangida (IBB), and Sani Abacha used the extensive emergency powers they granted themselves to rule by decree. What limited consultation took place, seldom, if ever, included ordinary people or their self-chosen representatives.

The situation has scarcely improved under the civilian leaders who have held power continuously since they reclaimed it in May 1999.[39] All too quickly, in fact, the hope and expectation that accompanied Obasanjo's election as president gave way first to alarm and then dejection. The gloom was lifted slightly by his failure to secure a third term in office and his eventual, albeit reluctant, surrender of power to Yar'Adua, who noisily declared his enthusiasm for the rule of law. But he has since returned with a vengeance, and continues to deepen the longer Yar'Adua's presidency lasts, as he stubbornly refuses to display any such commitment to due process. Indeed, he has succeeded, along with his predecessor, in transforming Nigeria into a *de facto* one party state in which the electoral process is now so compromised that anyone who hopes to hold office cannot afford to allow elections to proceed unimpeded.

Today, the People's Democratic Party (PDP) dominates Nigerian politics in a way in which no other party has in the past. Even under the First Republic — the only other period in Nigeria's history when civilians held power for a comparable length of time— the elected representatives were divided far more equitably between the various parties. A majority were members of the Northern People's Congress (NPC). But a large minority belonged to the Action Group (AG), the National Convention of Nigerian Citizens (NCNC), the Nigerian National Democratic Party (NNDP), and the United Progressive Grand Alliance (UPGA). Now though, political life at the federal, state and local levels is dominated by the PDP. In addition to both the president and vice-president, 28 of the country's 36 state governors are PDP men, as are most members of the various state assemblies and local government areas.

This dominance would be less worrying, although still far from ideal, if PDP membership was not now a vital prerequisite for candidates seeking public office and especially high office. Indeed, the PDP exploits its large size to make sure, by both fair means and foul, that its people "win." For example, the violence that gripped the city of Jos, in November 2008 was initially triggered by the PDP's rigging of the ballot in a local election to ensure that its candidate (a Christian) won in an exclusively Muslim ward.[40] Time and again over the past decade, in fact, it has rigged national, state and local elections held all over the country.

This practice has become steadily more entrenched in the months since the presidential election of May 2007. It, too, was rigged by the PDP to ensure that Yar'Adua, Obasanjo's chosen successor, beat his two main rivals, Atiku Abubakar (Obasanjo's former vice-president) and Muhammadu Buhari (the former military dictator). According to most accounts, the election was anything but free and fair. During the build up to the election, the U.S. State Department issued its annual human rights report on Nigeria. It observed that the Nigerian police routinely, and often violently, harassed opposition candidates and their supporters; that the authorities obstructed and illegally detained journalists; that government agents were involved in politically motivated murders; and that vigilante groups were hired by incumbent politicians to intimidate their rivals.[41]

Of the election itself, the European Union's (EU) observation mission noted that "polling procedures were often poorly followed and the secrecy of the vote was not guaranteed in the majority of . . . stations," as well as many instances "of fraud, including ballot box stuffing, multiple voting, intimidation of voters, alteration of official result forms, stealing of sensitive polling materials, vote buying and under age voting."[42] These criticisms were echoed by the United Nations (UN), Amnesty International, and Human Rights Watch. Indeed, it "observed violence and intimidation . . . in an electoral process that denied large numbers of voters the opportunity to cast their votes." And "where voting did occur, it was marred by the late opening of polls, a severe shortage of ballot papers, the widespread intimidation of voters, the seizure of ballot boxes by gangs of thugs, vote buying and other irregularities."[43]

Not long after Yar'Adua's victory was declared, both Atiku and Buhari launched separate legal challenges to have it overturned. To hear their cases, a special tribunal of five judges was convened. As well as deciding whether any fraud had been committed, it was the panel's task to determine what should be done if it had. After months of deliberation, it finally delivered its unanimous verdict on February 26, 2008, and found against both plaintiffs. Within hours of the announcement of its judgement, rumours began to circulate of massive payments made to its members by a third party close to Obasanjo. It was alleged that in return for this money, which amounted to hundreds of millions of *naira*, the five Justices were expected to dismiss both cases.

Unexpectedly perhaps, given that Yar'Adua is from Katsina, this outcome was only lukewarmly received in the north. Prior to the election, he was largely unknown throughout the region. And those who had heard of him usually knew him as Shehu's younger brother.[44] He was certainly far less high profile than either Atiku or Buhari, who are also northerners. Quite rightly, given their long involvement in national politics, they are seen as two of Nigeria's most senior statesmen. And even though the PDP is the party of the current northern-dominated administration, it does not command universal support throughout the region. Indeed, three of the eight states with non-PDP governors, Borno, Kaduna, and Yobe, are in the north. Their governors, Ali Modu Sheriff, Ibrahim Shekharau and Ibrahim Geidam, belong to the All Nigeria Peoples Party (ANPP), for which Buhari stood in the 2007 presidential election.

The north, therefore, is no more immune to the feelings of political disenfranchisement that are currently swirling around the country than anywhere else. In fact, that a northern administration has failed so completely to even begin to tackle the region's many economic and social problems only compounds the disappointment felt by many of those who live there. For in a clinentelist state such as Nigeria, ties of blood and religion are supposed to matter. Yet seemingly they do not, which makes the general inability of ordinary voters to hold their political leaders to account, and if necessary change them, all the more frustrating.

And this sense of marginalization continues to be heightened by the state's routine abuse of human rights and the violence with which it often responds to popular protests. The past 12 months have witnessed a procession of bloody riots as Nigerians, usually young men, take to the streets to make their displeasure known. That there have been so many demonstrations such as these speaks volumes about the limited opportunities ordinary people have to make themselves heard or get involved in the political process. The majority of these disturbances occurred in the north, in the cities of Jos (November 2008), Bauchi (February 2009), Zaria (June 2009), Kano (July 2009), Maidugiri (July 2009), and Bauchi again (August 2009).

On each occasion, the state's response was ferocious. In Jos, the local governor ordered the police and army to simply shoot suspected rioters on sight.[45] According to the most up-to-date estimates, some 700 people (most of them protestors) died during this crackdown.[46] More recently, the leader of the *Boko Haram* group, Mohammed Yusuf, was summarily executed by MOPOL officers for orchestrating violent demonstrations in several northern cities.[47] While his death was warmly welcomed by President Yar'Adua's administration,[48] it caused consternation among human rights groups and ordinary Nigerians. To them, the state's treatment of Yusuf and the Jos protestors highlights both its absolute refusal to brook any dissent, and its determination to close off the few remaining avenues for the general public to make its views known.

That taking to the streets is now one of the only ways ordinary people can hope to influence the political debate helps explain the vehemence and violence of so many demonstrations. Their protests are given added urgency by the abject poverty in which the vast majority of them live. It is with undiluted desperation that these people call on their political leaders to help them in their daily struggle for survival. They are, in fact, emissaries for the masses with whom they share the same problems and anxieties. In 2005, 92 percent of all men, women, and children lived on $2 or less a day, and 70 percent on $1 or less.[49] This extremely high rate of poverty has been brought about by three distinct processes: Nigeria's transformation into a rentier state; the failure of its economic growth to keep pace with demographic growth; and the increasing concentration of the wealth that is generated in the hands of a few.

Nigeria's evolution into a rentier state is directly tied to the development of its oil industry. It has grown rapidly over the past 40 years and has turned the country into one of the world's most important energy suppliers. In 1960 Nigeria extracted around 20,000 barrels of crude a day, which represented just 0.09 percent of the total amount produced worldwide. By 1971, the year in which it joined the OPEC, these figures had jumped to 1.1 million and 2.25 percent, respectively. And today, it produces something in the region of 2.2 million barrels a day, or 3 percent of the total amount extracted worldwide.[50]

Yet even this remarkable growth pales in comparison to the speed with which Nigeria now so completely depends on its oil revenue. In 1960 the 2.4 billion *naira* the country netted from its sale of oil abroad represented just 2.7 percent of its total export earnings. By 1980, such sales (which were worth 12,791.7 billion *naira*) made up a staggering 96.1 percent of its export income.[51] Even today, these proceeds are the mainstay of its export and foreign currency earnings. So much so, that both its economy and the government's spending plans are totally reliant upon them. Nigeria's future prosperity and public services, therefore, depend on a market that is notoriously volatile.

This exposure has been made all the more complete by the federal and state governments' failure to adequately maintain their tax collection capabilities. Arguably, this is one of the very few ways in which ordinary Nigerians benefit from their country's oil windfall. Using such revenue to alleviate the popular tax burden, is a well-established practice and has been adopted by the governments of oil producing countries the world over. Yet for Nigerians—just as for Saudi Arabians, Kuwaitis, Bahrainis, and Bruneians—this arrangement is something of a Faustian pact, for it makes their political leaders even less inclined to pay them any heed. Indeed, since the tax they pay is so inconsequential, their governments are less beholden to them.

The rapid and massive expansion of Nigeria's oil industry has also stymied the growth of its economy. For like many other countries that earn a significant portion of their income from the sale of this or that natural resource, Nigeria has succumbed to the Dutch Disease. Coined in the late 1970s by the *Economist* magazine to explain the collapse of manufacturing in the Netherlands following its discovery of natural gas a decade earlier, the term refers to those instances when a country suffers from exchange rate problems resulting from its sudden overdependence on the export of a single commodity, usually an unrefined or unprocessed natural resource of some description.[52]

In the case of Nigeria, the country was flooded with foreign currency, which raised the value of the *naira* to artificially high levels. As a result, imported goods were much cheaper and were highly sought after by the *nouveaux riches* because of the status attached to them. This led to a decrease in demand for local agricultural and manufactured products, sending these sectors of the economy into decline. Their collapse has been hastened by the flight of huge numbers of people from the countryside to the cities as they seek to make their fortunes on the back of the oil bonanza. As a result, the country's economy contracted by an average of -0.1 percent per annum between 1975 and 2005.[53]

Unsurprisingly, this prolonged period of stagnation has had a devastating effect on the livelihoods and standards of living of many ordinary Nigerians. One of the most pressing problems is perennial un- and underemployment. As it is, there are no accurate statistics as to what proportion of the labor force is either out of work, working part-time, or working in the informal economy. Sheikh Kabara estimates that between 70 and 80 percent of the workforce in northern Nigeria is unemployed.[54] While he has no hard data to back this claim, his is an informed opinion based on what he sees and hears daily. Moreover, it broadly tallies with the best guesses of the UN, International Monetary Fund (IMF), and World Bank, which suspect that the rate of jobless in the region is extremely high.

One of the main reasons there is so much unemployment in the north is because the number of people looking for work keeps increasing. Needless to say, the size of Nigeria's labor pool is directly linked to the rate at which its population continues to grow. And over the past 25 years, Nigeria's population has grown exponentially. Indeed in 1975, it stood at 61.2 million people. By 2005 though, it had more than doubled to 141.4 million people, and it is projected to rise to 175.7 million people by 2015. This means that between 1975 and 2005, the country's population grew at a staggering 2.8 percent a year. And between 2005 and 2015, it is set to grow by a similarly remarkable 2.2 percent annually.[55]

Each and every year, then, hundreds of thousands of young people join the labor market for the first time. So many, in fact, that even a dynamic expanding economy would struggle to find gainful employment for them all, and Nigeria's economy is anything but dynamic. There are, in short, far too many people chasing far too few jobs, and there is little prospect of this high demographic growth rate slowing significantly anytime soon. Indeed, for cultural and domestic and international political reasons, Nigeria's politicians are ill inclined to even try to limit it.

The hardships imposed on the mass of ordinary people by Nigeria's poor economic performance continue to be compounded by rampant corruption. Sadly, Nigeria's reputation as a den of iniquity is thoroughly deserved. In its 2007 *Global Corruption Barometer*, Transparency International placed Nigeria in the top quintile of countries most affected by bribery.[56] And in its 2008 *Corruption Perceptions Index*, it ranked Nigeria 121st out of 180 countries (with the first placed country being the least corrupt and the last the most).[57] One of the most devastating consequences of corruption is the damage it inflicts on public services. To begin with, right at the start of the funding chain, high level politicians and officials siphon off huge sums of money to line their own pockets and maintain the clientelist networks that help keep them in power. From the outset, therefore, the health, education, infrastructure, and other budgets are reduced in size to the detriment of those who depend on the services they are supposed to fund.

The money that is spent is often poorly invested, as these same politicians and officials use their privileged positions to award lucrative public works contracts to companies owned by friends and relations. As a result, the public rarely gets good value for money, as it is forced to pay over the odds for the work that is undertaken. All too often, that which is carried out is substandard, as middlemen and contractors cut corners in order to reduce costs and maximize their profits. And, finally, at the other end of the funding chain, the low level officials and state employees, whose task it is to deliver these services, habitually demand additional payments from those requesting their help. Sometimes these demands are motivated by greed, but on other occasions they are driven by necessity, as these employees are forced to supplement their meagre and erratically paid salaries.

The ineffectiveness of Nigeria's public services is highlighted by their continued failure to adequately meet the needs of ordinary people. This accusation is not unusual and is frequently levelled against service providers the world over. Yet it is the degree of shortfall between what those in Nigeria offer and what is actually needed that, in this case, makes this criticism both legitimate and so concerning. Indeed, the latest data on the state of the Nigerian nation's health and education is extremely worrying. First and foremost, the average life expectancy of its members currently stands at just 46.5 years, and is only slightly higher than it was in 1970 after 3 years of brutal civil war.[58] This average continues to be dragged down by the high rates of infant and maternal mortality. Out of every 1,000 children born in the country, 201 will not live to see their 5th birthday. Out of every 100,000 expectant mothers, 800 will die giving birth.[59]

But more broadly, tens of millions of Nigerians continue to endure general ill health brought on by a lack of access to clean drinking water, adequate medical care, and food that is sufficiently nutritious. Indeed, one-in-two (52 percent) is forced to drink water that is not safe, while one-in-three (34 percent) cannot attain sufficient calories each day even when all income is spent on food alone.[60] As of 2004, for every 100,000 people there were just 28 doctors,[61] most of whom were clustered in the major towns and cities, far removed from the rural masses. Indeed, in the remoter districts of the Niger Delta and the far north, health care provision is virtually nonexistent.

The failure of the federal, state, and local authorities to maintain these services gives rise to feelings of both anger and resignation among ordinary Nigerians. Many are outraged by the authorities' disinterested incompetence and their seeming total inability to get anything to work properly. Their fury is stoked by the corruption that continues to deprive the public sector of millions of dollars of much needed funding. But many others have simply given up. For as long as they can remember, these services have never really worked; so long in fact, they have renounced all hope that someday such services might work. In different ways, both these emotions help make the propagation of radical Islamist ideas easier. Those who are angry are susceptible because the Islamist groups who propagate these ideas seem to share their indignation, while promising to punish the guilty. And those who are resigned are grateful to anyone for whatever help and hope they can offer. In Nigeria as elsewhere, *salafist* groups have shown themselves adept at adapting their arguments and methods when courting different constituencies.

Conclusions and Recommendations.

The challenges the *Izala*, IMN, MIR, and *Boko Haram* present the *Qadiriyya* and *Tijaniyya* have led them to add another dimension to the various community outreach programs they each run. There is little doubt that these programs are central to the Brotherhoods' efforts to attract new followers and to improve the lives of existing members and the wider community. Yet unavoidably (although not unintentionally) they have assumed another purpose; to stop individuals from joining or supporting one of the radical Islamic groups. This suggests that the rivalry between the *Qadiriyya* and *Tijaniyya* and the Islamist groups is mostly zero-sum. A triumph for one represents a defeat for the other; the recruitment of an individual means there is one less person who can support their adversary. On no account can there be mutually assisted growth.

That it is this way is mainly the result of the antagonistic positions they have each adopted in relation to the other. Indeed, part of the *Izala's raison d'être* is to confront *Sufism*. Yet the collision this invites is made all the more certain by the fragility of what can be termed the middle ground. To claim that there is no third way would be untrue. In fact, there are various alternatives to siding with either the Brotherhoods or Islamist groups. These include supporting the Sultan,

Emirs, and other traditional rulers, following a different religion, or simply remaining neutral. It is possible to pursue several of these paths consecutively. Rare is the member of the *Tijaniyya* who does not also recognize the authority of the Sultan or *Emirs* of Kano, Zaria Katsina, and so on. Many Christians in the north still acknowledge the historic roles performed by these rulers and their continued politico-religious importance.

Yet even so, the weakness of the north's economy allied to the failure of the federal, state, and local authorities to provide meaningful social services and the persistence of corruption, often forces people to take sides. Indeed, they frequently do so for no other reason than to gain access to the welfare provisions made by the various organizations. This makes no mention of those who actually agree with what these groups argue and seek to achieve, or their explanations of what measures need to be taken to make the lives of northern Nigeria's inhabitants better. Moreover, the failings of the federal, state, and local governments do little but destroy popular confidence in both secularism and democracy. Why support a political system that has failed so completely to improve peoples' lives and has now become so corrupted that it is arguably an obstacle to progress?

Given, then, that the political, economic, and social conditions in northern Nigeria are currently so conducive of Islamic radicalism, the challenge confronting the United States and the broader international community is as great as it is urgent. Without doubt, its ultimate goal must be to encourage the implementation of reforms to eliminate these conditions. As elsewhere throughout the Islamic world, the promotion of good governance and economic prosperity holds the key to achieving a lasting solution. Yet as past experience shows, this is often difficult to accomplish. Not least, because the political leaders and governing elites the international community has to engage with are frequently the very people who have the most to gain from perpetuating the status quo.

In the meantime, help must be granted to those organizations, like the *Qadiriyya* and *Tijaniyya*, which are working to counteract the Islamists' siren call. This not only helps strengthen civil society— so vital to creating a well governed state and vibrant democracy— but also acts as a bulwark against the further spread of Islamist ideals and groups. The first and most obvious observation that can be made of these short- and long-term measures is that they require the United States and its allies—most notably Britain, France and the EU—to become far more actively engaged in and with Nigeria. For quite clearly the diplomatic, economic, and military investment that is currently being made is insufficient (even if it has steadily increased since the restoration of civilian rule). Indeed, the failure of this support is reinforced by the Fund for Peace research institute's recent forecast that Nigeria will become a failed state sometime during the next decade.[62]

Yet how can the *Qadiriyya* and *Tijaniyya* best be supported? And more broadly, how can the United States engage in and with Nigeria more effectively? One potential course of action, which has the added benefit of raising the U.S. profile in the north, is to establish a permanent consular presence in a major northern urban center (preferably Kano). For a start, this building and its staff would serve as a constant reminder of the U.S. commitment to both the country and the region. In addition, it would provide a focal point through which aid, development assistance, and military training could be channelled. In this way, the United States could extend its influence throughout the region and into the southern *Sahel*.

The consul therefore, would be able to complement the activities of the U.S. Ambassador in Abuja and assist the MPRI contractors working at the Armed Forces Command and Staff College in Jaji. It could also support the activities of the TSCTI team operating out of Timbuktu in neighbouring Mali. Indeed, the establishment of a permanent consular presence in the north would fill an increasingly significant gap in the U.S. capabilities in the region. It would make up for the declining influence of its close ally, Britain. Its official residence in Kaduna is a useful base but is not permanently manned by consular staff. It is gradually winding down its Defence Advisory Team (BDAT), and is still debating whether or not to replace its Honorary Consul, who died in early 2009.

In addition to setting up a permanent mission in the north, there are other useful measures the U.S. Government can take to assist the *Qadiriyya* and *Tijaniyya*. These include: providing both Brotherhoods with economic assistance to finance their education programs; providing them with up-to-date learning materials; encouraging U.S. schools and colleges to set up staff and student exchange programs; encouraging them to cooperate more frequently, and to a greater extent, with one another; and encouraging them to strengthen their ties with the Sultan and *Emirs*. Yet important questions still remain as to how this assistance can best be delivered. Why, for example, would the Nigerian government allow the United States to deal directly with the Brotherhoods? If it refuses to grant such access, how should the United States respond? Should it try to provide this help covertly? If so, how?

Of course, it is in everyone's best interests for the

United States to operate openly. That way, it avoids upsetting the Nigerian government, is able to provide the Brotherhoods with greater assistance, and can incorporate its provision within a public relations campaign aimed at improving the U.S. image within the Islamic world. Yet this openness should not be attempted at all costs. Clearly, if this means funnelling yet more money to Nigerian state institutions, which are hopelessly corrupt, then it should be avoided, for that would simply be a waste of U.S. tax dollars. Rather, the United States should strive to forge a direct relationship with the Brotherhoods, one that bypasses the Nigerian state's ineffective and unreliable organs.

Given the FG's seeming disinterest in the well-being of its citizens, this may well be possible. Certainly its officials have yet to complain about the money spent by the British government on the Sultan of Sokoto and Sheikh Kabara, and given to the *Emir* of Zaria. Indeed, over the past 2 or 3 years, it has paid for both the Sultan and the Sheikh to visit the UK on at least two separate occasions each. It is helping to finance the restoration of the ornate gatehouse that formed part of the ancient city walls of Zaria. And it has also paid for various conferences and other civic events to which the north's religious leaders have been invited as guests of honor.

The funding for these initiatives came from schemes organized by the High Commission, and are separate from the much larger programs managed by the UK's Department for International Development (DFID). As a result, the sums involved are not that great. Arguably, this may explain why the Nigerian government appears so unconcerned. Yet there are still important lessons to draw. For a start, there is the precedent these initiatives help establish. Even though they are small, they establish a pattern by which the British government deals directly with the Brotherhoods to pursue its socio-political objectives. Then, there is the example they set. By dividing funding between various schemes so that none is very large, the U.S. Government might be able to give significant assistance to the Brotherhoods without drawing too much attention to the fact that it is doing so.

Any such attempts to deal directly with the *Qadiriyya* and *Tijaniyya* are also likely to benefit from the high standing both Brotherhoods enjoy within northern Nigerian society. Indeed, the wide respect they command means that Nigeria's political leaders are unlikely to complain about any assistance given them. To a certain degree, these politicians are keen both to keep the *Qadiriyya* and *Tijaniyya* on side and be associated with them. In fact, perhaps the most significant obstacle that would need to be negotiated is Nigeria's Christian community. For it mostly sees itself as being in competition with its Muslim counterpart and would, in all likelihood, be upset if it felt that the other was being given preferential treatment by the United States.

Questions still remain as to whether the *Qadiriyya* and *Tijaniyya* would accept any help offered by the United States. It is not inconceivable that they might reject it for fear of undermining the loyalty of their members and standing within the wider community. It must be acknowledged that the United States is viewed with considerable suspicion by many throughout the Islamic world. Invariably, this opposition is justified on the grounds that the United States is purportedly hostile toward Muslims, their governments, and even Islam. Those making such claims substantiate them by pointing to the difficult relations the United States has with Libya, Sudan, Syria, and Iran; its recent invasions of Afghanistan and Iraq; and its strong support of Israel. Certainly, some Nigerian Muslims are critical of the United States and its foreign policy for these very reasons.

Yet on the whole, northern Nigerians are not as opposed to the United States as some of their co-religionists elsewhere in the Islamic world.[63] That this is so should not come as a surprise, given the affection the Sultan, *Emirs*, *Qadiriyya* and *Tijaniyya* still feel toward Britain, one of the closest allies of the United States. In fact, both Sheikh Kabara and Sheikh Khalifa have appeared in public with members of the British High Commission numerous times to thank them for the assistance they periodically provide and to call on London to offer more. Sheikh Kabara makes no secret of the fact that his son is currently studying in the UK. Indeed, the Brotherhoods' willingness to receive this assistance, and their openness when doing so, is encouraging, as it suggests that they are likely to be receptive to any help the United States might want to offer.

Britain's efforts to maintain and strengthen its relationships with the *Qadiriyya* and *Tijaniyya* are led by its High Commission in Abuja. In turn, the High Commission looks to its Northern Affairs officer to take primary responsibility for this task. Their duties, like those of their counterpart in the U.S. Embassy, are extremely broad. They have to monitor and report on all major political, economic, social, and cultural developments in the north. Unsurprisingly, these responsibilities require the officer to travel extensively throughout the region and meet with key local figures including Sheikh Kabara and Sheikh Khalifa. In this way, the British government is able to retain contact and remain on good relations with both Brotherhoods.

The Northern Officer's efforts are supplemented

by other measures. To begin with, the High Commissioner and other senior members of the British mission periodically travel to Kano and meet with both Sheikhs. Often when they do, they are accompanied by important visitors from London, including Members of Parliament and government ministers. That these high ranking officials take the time and effort to meet with them is greatly appreciated by Sheikh Kabara and Sheikh Khalifa, as are the official visits to the UK that the High Commission organizes on their behalf. During the course of these trips, both Sheikhs meet with political and religious leaders. Such meetings not only help strengthen Britain's relations with both men, but also enable the British government to discuss more carefully with them what it wants to achieve in northern Nigeria.

Of course, the British High Commission is not alone in pursuing such initiatives. Other missions, including the U.S. Embassy, adopt similar practices. And for good reason, as the diplomatic value of direct and frequent contact cannot be overemphasised. As well as demonstrating both the U.S. commitment to the Brotherhoods and desire to work them, such cooperation also bestows on them a degree of prestige as a partner of choice of the U.S. Government. Arguably, it is in the area of diplomacy that the U.S. military can make its greatest contributions, as the defense attaché and staff have an important role to play in maintaining and strengthening the U.S. Embassy's relations with the Brotherhoods.

In addition to this political function, the U.S. military can also help by offering to reform Nigeria's security sector. Without a doubt, the actions of its armed forces and police continue to drive northern Muslims into the open arms of radical Islamic groups. To begin, the brutality with which the army and MOPOL invariably respond to demonstrations and protests causes both outrage and consternation among ordinary Nigerians. So much so, that it leaves some sections of society, unemployed young men in particular, vulnerable and exposed to the Islamists' siren calls. Even more fundamentally, the army should not be required to provide everyday policing on the scale that it does. It does not possess the necessary skills to properly investigate and monitor such groups.

ENDNOTES

1. Daniel Jordan Smith, *A Culture of Corruption: Everyday Deceit and Popular Discontent in Nigeria*, Princeton, NJ, and Oxford, UK: Princeton University Press, 2007, p. 5.

2. These churches are so-called because that is what those who preach in them offer their congregations.

3. John N. Paden, *Faith and Politics in Nigeria*, Washington DC: United States Institute of Peace Press, 2008, p. 3.

4. So-called radical Islamic groups have been identified in northern Nigeria for much of the past century. This description was first applied to selected bodies and organizations by the British, who governed the region from 1900 to 1960. Yet the criteria used by British officials to determine whether a group was radical or not were markedly different from those employed today. Whereas now individuals and groups are labelled radical because of their views on democracy, human rights, and the use of violence to achieve socio-political ends, during the colonial era factions were categorized as radical on the basis of their attitude toward British rule.

5. *Salafism*'s emphasis on doctrinal orthodoxy contrasts "markedly with the strong elements of mysticism and doctrinal eclecticism found within traditional . . . Islam of the Marabouts and the Sufi Brotherhoods. *Salafists* believe that *Sufi* 'practices

and traditions [are] alien to Islam primarily because of their emphasis on intermediaries between God and Man, and [lead] to decadence and superstition." Michael Willis, *The Islamist Challenge in Algeria: A Political History*, Reading, NY: Ithaca Press, 1996, pp. 12 -13.

6. The continent's other major oil producers are Algeria, Angola, and Libya.

7. Sonia Shah, *Crude: The Story of Oil*, New York: Seven Stories Press, 2004, p. 94.

8. U.S. Department of States, "Background Note: Nigeria," September 2009, available from *www.state.gov/r/pa/ei/bgn/2836. htm.*

9. J. N. C Hill, *Identity in Algerian Politics: The Legacy of Colonial Rule*, Boulder, CO: Lynne Rienner Publishers, 2009, p. 180.

10. *Ibid.*, p. 176.

11. By this time, the GSPC was already making overtures to Al Qaeda. These links were made more formal in September 2006 when Abdelmalek Droukdel, the GSPC's *emir*, announced an alliance between the two groups. Finally, in January 2007, he announced that, in recognition of this new union, the GSPC would forthwith be known as *Al Qaeda in the Land of the Islamic Maghreb.*

12. These neighbors include Sierra Leone, Liberia, Cote d'Ivoire, Niger, and the Democratic Republic of the Congo (DRC).

13. Martin Evans and John Philips, *Algeria: The Anger of the Dispossessed*, New Haven, CT, and London, UK: 2007, p. 287.

14. The DSCA's budget for 2009 was $750 million. Department of Defense, "Fiscal Year (FY) 2009 Budget Estimates Defense Security Cooperation Agency (DSCA)," 2009, available from *www. defenselink.mil/comptroller/defbudget/fy2009/budget_justification/ pdfs/01_Operation_and_Maintenance/O_M_VOL_1_PARTS/ DSCA%20FY%2009%20PB%20OP-5.pdf.*

15. John N. Paden, *Muslim Civic Cultures and Conflict Resolution: The Challenge of Democratic Federalism in Nigeria,* Washington DC, Brookings Institution Press: 2005, p. 253 n 5.

16. Indeed, according to intelligence reports drafted by the colonial authorities in the early 20th century, the Brotherhoods were viewed as focal points for opposition and resistance to British rule.

17. John Esposito, ed., *The Oxford Encyclopaedia of the Modern Islamic World,* 4th Ed., Oxford, UK: Oxford University Press, 1995, p. 105.

18. A.J. Arberry, *Sufism: An Account of the Mystics of Islam,* New York: Dover Publications Inc., p. 35.

19. This coolness in the relations between the *Qadiriyya* and *Tijaniyya* became apparent during the course of my interviews with Sheikh Kabara and Sheikh Khalifa.

20. Paden, *Faith and Politics in Nigeria,* p. 28.

21. Ousmane Kane, *Muslim Modernity in Postcolonial Nigeria: A Study of the Society for the Removal of Innovation and Reinstatement of Tradition,* Leiden and Boston, MA: Brill, 2003, p. 232.

22. John L. Esposito, *Islam and Politics,* 4th Ed., New York: Syracuse University Press, 1984, p. 37.

23. Qaribullahi Sheikh Nasir Kabara, Leader of Qadiriyya in Nigeria and West Africa, interview by author, Sheikh Kabara's home in Kano Nigeria, February 26, 2009; and Sheikh Ismail Ibrahim Khalifa, Leader of Tijaniyya in Nigeria and West Africa, interview by author, Sheikh Khalifa's home in Kano, Nigeria, June 11, 2009.

24. Paden, *Faith and Politics in Nigeria,* p. 30.

25. Toyin Falola, *Violence in Nigeria: The Crisis of Religious Politics and Secular Ideologies,* Rochester, NY: Rochester University Press, 1998, p. 195.

26. Karl Maier, *This House Has Fallen*, London, UK: Penguin Books, 2000, p. 175.

27. *Ibid.*, p. 166.

28. See for example, Zakzaky's long defense of Bin Laden. Mallam Ibraheem Zakzaky, "Terrorism in the World Today, What is Terrorism? Who are the Terrorists?" 2009, available from *www. islamicmovement.org/sheikh/terrorism2.htm.*

29. Islamic Movement in Nigeria, "Activities," 2009, available from *www.islamicmovement.org/activities.htm.*

30. Indeed one after another from 1999 onwards, the 12 states that make up the north adopted *sharia* law.

31. Islamic Movement in Nigeria, "Activities," p. 1.

32. Kabara, interview by author; and Khalifa, interview by author.

33. Khalifa, interview by author.

34. Paden, *Muslim Civic Cultures and Conflict Resolution*, p. 188.

35. This Day, "Boko Haram—Death Toll Now 700, Says Security Commander," August 2, 2009, available from *allafrica. com/stories/200908020001.html*, p. 1.

36. This is certainly the view of Ahmed Nuhu, a descendent of a former Emir of Zaria and possible successor to the current incumbent. Ahmed Nuhu, interview by author Abuja, Nigeria, December 5, 2008.

37. From October 1, 1960, to August 16, 1963, Nigeria had three regions—Northern, Western, and Eastern. Following a referendum held on July 13, 1963, a fourth region—Mid-Western—was created out of the Western region. Benjamin Obi Nwabueze, *A Constitutional History of Nigeria*, London, UK: Hurst, 1982, pp. 136-137.

38. Jean Herskovits, "Nigeria's Rigged Democracy," *Foreign Affairs*, Vol. 86, No. 4, July/August 2007, p. 120.

39. Indeed, in 2007 Human Rights Watch stated that "Nigeria has not held a free and fair general election since the end of military rule." Human Rights Watch, "Election or 'Selection'? Human Rights Abuses and Threats to Free and Fair Elections in Nigeria," April 4, 2007, available from *www.unhcr.org/refworld/docid/463732ec2.html*.

40. BBC, "Nigeria Riot Victims Swamp Medics," December 1, 2008, p. 1, available from *news.bbc.co.uk/1/hi/world/africa/7758098.stm*.

41. U.S. State Department, "Nigeria," *Country Report on Human Rights Practices 2006.*

42. European Election Observation Mission, "Nigeria Final Report: Gubernatorial and State Houses of Assembly Elections 14 April 2007 and Presidential and National Assembly Elections 21 April 2007," August 23, 2007, p. 4, available from *ec.europa.eu/external_relations/human_rights/eu_election_ass_observ/nigeria/report_final_annex_23-08-07_en.pdf*.

43. Human Rights Watch, "Nigeria: Presidential Election Marred by Fraud, Violence," April 25, 2007, p. 1, available from *www.hrw.org/en/news/2007/04/24/nigeria-presidential-election-marred-fraud-violence*.

44. Shehu Yar'Adua had been an army officer before moving into politics. Unlike his brother, he was both charismatic and gregarious until his untimely death in one of Sani Abacha's prisons.

45. Human Rights Watch, "Nigeria: Arbitrary Killings by Security Forces in Jos," December 19, 2008, p. 1, available from *www.hrw.org/en/news/2008/12/19/nigeria-arbitrary-killings-security-forces-jos*.

46. Human Rights Watch, "Arbitrary Killings by Security Forces Submission to the Investigative Bodies on the November 28-29, 2008 Violence in Jos, Plateau State, Nigeria," July 2009, p. 1, available from *www.unhcr.org/refworld/pdfid/4a641c0e2.pdf*.

47. He was shot and killed while in police custody on July 30, 2009.

48. Indeed, his Information Minister, Dora Akunyili, went so far as to describe Yusuf's death as "the best thing that could have happened to Nigeria." Agence France-Presse, "Sect Leader's Death Best Thing for Nigeria: Minister," July 31, 2009.

49. United Nations, "2007/2008 Human Development Report," 2008, p. 1, available from *hdrstats.undp.org/countries/data_sheets/cty_ds_NGA.html*.

50. Andy Rowell, James Marriott, and Lorne Stockman, *The Next Gulf*, London, UK: Constable, 2005, p. 105.

51. Olayiwola Abegunrin, *Nigerian Foreign Policy under Military Rule, 1966-1999*, Westport, CT, and London, UK: Praeger, 2003, p. 169.

52. John Ghazvinian, *Untapped: The Scramble for Africa's Oil*, London, UK: Harcourt, 2007, pp. 96-98.

53. United Nations, "2007/2008 Human Development Report," p. 1.

54. Kabara, interview by author.

55. United Nations, "2007/2008 Human Development Report," p. 1.

56. Transparency International," Global Corruption Barometer," 2007, available from *www.transparency.org*.

57. Transparency International, "2008 Corruption Perceptions Index," 2008, available from *www.transparency.org/news_room/in_focus/2008/cpi2008/cpi_2008_table*.

58. Then it stood at 42.8 years. United Nations, "2007/2008 Human Development Report," 2008, p. 1, available from *hdrstats.undp.org/countries/data_sheets/cty_ds_NGA.html*.

59. Department for International Development, "Nigeria," June 2008, p. 1, available from *www.dfid.giv.uk/countries/africa/Nigeria-facts.asp*.

60. *Ibid.*

61. United Nations, "2007/2008 Human Development Report," p. 2.

62. Fund for Peace, "Failed States Index 2009," 2009, p. 1, available from *www.foreignpolicy.com/articles/2009/06/22/2009_ failed_states_index_interactive_map_and_rankings.*

63. Kabara, interview by author.

U.S. ARMY WAR COLLEGE

Major General Robert M. Williams
Commandant

*****

STRATEGIC STUDIES INSTITUTE

Director
Professor Douglas C. Lovelace, Jr.

Director of Research
Dr. Antulio J. Echevarria II

Author
Dr. J. N. C. Hill

Director of Publications
Dr. James G. Pierce

Publications Assistant
Ms. Rita A. Rummel

*****

Composition
Mrs. Jennifer E. Nevil

www.ingramcontent.com/pod-product-compliance
Lightning Source LLC
Chambersburg PA
CBHW071355310526
45790CB00017B/888